We Travel So Far...

A FIREFLY BOOK

Published by Firefly Books Ltd. 2018

Copyright © 2017 words & pictures

First printing

Publisher Cataloging-in-Publication Data (U.S.)

Library of Congress Control Number: 2017962742

Library and Archives Canada Cataloguing in Publication

Knowles, Laura, author
       We travel so far... / words by Laura Knowles ; pictures by Chris Madden.
ISBN 978-1-77085-985-2 (hardcover)
      1. Animal migration--Juvenile literature.
2. Animal migration--Pictorial works--Juvenile literature.
I. Madden, Chris (Illustrator), illustrator II. Title.
QL754.K66 2018   j591.56'8   C2017-907767-8

Published in the United States by
Firefly Books (U.S.) Inc.
P.O. Box 1338, Ellicott Station
Buffalo, New York 14205

Published in Canada by
Firefly Books Ltd.
50 Staples Avenue, Unit 1
Richmond Hill, Ontario L4B 0A7

Printed in China

First published by words & pictures
Part of The Quarto Group
The Old Brewery, 6 Blundell Street,
London, N7 9BH

For Abi & Elliot,
my whole world.
I love you.
C.M.

For my friends and
family far away.
L.K.

We Travel So Far...

Words by Laura Knowles
Pictures by Chris Madden

FIREFLY BOOKS

CONTENTS

A True Story

Each story in this book is true. They are stories of incredible animal journeys; underwater, through the air, and over land.

These are the sort of journeys that we call "migration."

Often, animals migrate with the changing seasons. Some travel to find food, while others are driven to migrate to the perfect place to mate and raise their babies. For most migrating animals, all these reasons play a part.

The urge to migrate is instinctive:
it is hard-wired in them from
the moment they are born.

This book contains the stories of only
some of planet Earth's migrating animals,
but there are many others that also travel
amazing distances every year.

Next time you see a bird flying overhead,
just think—it might have flown all
the way from South America!

We are the
Leatherback Turtles.

We are record-breaking ocean swimmers.

We travel as far as 6,000 miles (10,000 km) in search of clouds of delicious jellyfish.

No one knows how we do it, but after all our ocean roving, we can find our way back to the same beach where we were born years before, ready to lay our own eggs there.

We are the **Humpback Whales**.

The long-way swimmers,
the ocean rovers.

In winter, we swim to the warm, tropical seas.

It's the perfect place for our babies to be born.

But when summer comes,
we journey to the icy polar waters.

Then we feast on tiny fish
and krill and fatten up for
another year.

We are the Sockeye Salmon,
the slippery, shimmery salmon.

We've traveled across the ocean, making our
way home to the rivers where we hatched.

Now we must swim against the current,

up the waterfalls,

through the raging rapids,

and past the hungry bears!

When we reach the shallow, gentle streams, we'll lay our eggs.

Our journey will be done, but new salmon will hatch and begin their own journey to the ocean.

We are the **Caribbean Spiny Lobsters**.

We live in shallow coastal waters.
We hide in cracks and crevices.
We like the warm, calm seas.

But as winter approaches,
so do the storms.

Quick!

We must travel into deep
water, where the water won't
be stirred up.

Our journey is quite a sight
to see. We link up into a long line
of spiky, seafloor scuttlers!

How do we find the way?
We have our own magnetic compass!

We are the **Elephant Seals**,
the blubber-buoyed ocean adventurers.

We make two migrations every year.

Over the winter, we give birth to our young,
up on the beaches of Mexico and California.

For three months, we live off our fat.
We become thin and hungry.

16

When spring arrives, we set off into
the North Pacific to find food.

We swim! We eat!

Mmm, it's good to grow fat again!

In summer, we journey back to our beaches,
where we shed our old hair and skin.

Now we're off again! Swimming to the
chilly north to feed before winter comes.

We are the **European Eels**.
We are the long, slippery swimmers.

For most of our lives we live in rivers.
We grow **big**,
we grow **old**,
and we **wait**.

On a dark autumn night, we begin our journey.
As we reach the salty coast, our eyes grow big
and our skin turns to shimmering silver.

We will swim all the way across the
mighty Atlantic Ocean, until we
reach the Sargasso Sea.

There we will lay our eggs.

Our eggs will hatch into larvae.

Eventually, the larvae will drift back to
the rivers and change into young eels,
ready to grow big, grow old, and wait.

We are the Ruby-throated Hummingbirds,

tiny bundles of nectar-fueled energy.

Though we weigh less than a nickel,
we fly as far as 7,400 miles (12,000 km) every year.

In spring, we fly up through eastern
North America, following the flowers.

In summer, we build nests
and raise our chicks.

By autumn, we must find more
food. We travel south to the
warmth of Central America.

We are the Wandering Albatrosses,
the long-winged wind riders.

We speed above the waves, we soar through the skies.

Across the stormy Southern Ocean,
we keep up our flight for hours on end.

We feed at night and rest on the ocean's choppy surface.
We only come back to land once every two years.

22

We each find our partner and, wings stretched wide, we dance the albatross dance.

We are the
Monarch
Butterflies.

We are clouds of fluttering, orange beauty.
Few other insects travel as far as we do.

At the end of summer,
fattened on nectar,
we swarm into the sky.

We make our way from Canada and northern U.S.,
down to the coasts of California and Mexico:
millions of butterflies, all traveling south.

When we reach our winter home,
we hang in clusters from the trees
and sleep until spring.

We are the **Whooping Cranes,**
the ghostly white fliers.

We travel the length of North America,
flying south for the winter.

Once, humans were our enemies, and
there were few of us left. We were
hunted and our habitat was taken.

Now, humans are our helpers.

It takes care, it takes time, but they are
teaching us the routes that cranes once flew.

We follow the whooping-crane
airplane across the wide, blue sky.

We are the
Fruit Bats.

We are the
nighttime flappers,
the sweet-treat
snackers!

We live in groups of
thousands, hanging
from the trees of Africa.

When the trees of Kasanka National Park are
heavy with fruit, we come from far and wide to feast.

Not a few, not a flock, but a mass of eight million bats!

We are the **Bar-headed Geese**.
We are the highest fliers!

Up in the clouds, the air is thin and cold.

There isn't much oxygen to breathe,
but still we keep on going.

We flap our wings for hours on end
as we race across the highest mountains.
All through the night we keep up our flight.

Our wings beat.

Beat.

Beat.

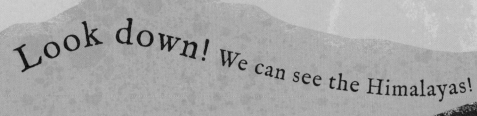

Look down! We can see the Himalayas!

We are the Desert Locusts,
a swarming sea of gobbling grasshoppers.

Normally, there are only few of us, living alone.

But when the rains come and
the crops are fresh and green,
our numbers suddenly grow.

All at once, there are
millions upon millions of us!
A whirring fog of insects!

We are so hungry; we fly
in search of food.

Wherever we travel, we strip the fields bare.

We are the Arctic Terns,
the daylight dancers.

We chase the summer,
pole to pole.

In the Arctic, we raise
our chicks.

Then we fly south with them to Antarctica.
There, we feast on fish and krill.

We are small, we are swift,
we travel the world.

We are the Zebras,
a sea of stripes on the Serengeti.

All our lives, we must keep on the move.

Our hooves take us to find new food.

With our strong teeth and stomachs,
we munch through the tough, dry grass.

Behind us, the fresh green shoots
are left for wildebeest and gazelle.

We are the **Wildebeests** of the African plains.
We follow the rains to where the
grass grows green.

Over the land—
watch out for lions!

Across the river—watch out for crocs!

With pounding hooves we keep up our march;
stumbling, rumbling, safety-in-numbering.

Wildebeests!
A million beasts!
As far as the eye can see!

We are the **Polar Bears**.

We've been waiting for winter.

We've been waiting for the sea ice to form.

Now we can journey across the ice sheets.

We can hunt in the freezing Arctic sea.

As we travel, our cubs will grow strong.

They will learn how to survive in this cold white world.

But if the world gets warmer, there will be no ice.
If there is no ice, there will be nowhere for us to hunt.

How will we survive in a warm, wet world?

We are the **Red Crabs,**
the land crabs, the rulers of Christmas Island.

We munch through leaves and seeds
on the rain forest floor.

It takes us a week to reach the coast:
waves of red meeting waves of blue.
Why have we come all this way?

To release our eggs at high tide, and let
them wash away into the salty sea.

When the autumn rains
arrive, it's time to go.

A sideways-scuttling,
red-river race to the sea!

We are the Garter Snakes.
We are the winter sleepers.

Every autumn, we travel to our underground holes.
We sleep through the cold season, hundreds of
snakes crammed in together.

When spring arrives, we come out
to warm our skin in the hot sun.

We're warm!
We're awake!
We are ready to mate.

Now it's time to slither back
to our summer home.

We live sheltered by grass and
shrubs, close to ponds and streams.

We don't travel as far as some animals, but
we make our journey like clockwork. A carpet
of sunbathing snakes is quite a sight to see!

We are the **Caribou**,
the thick-furred travelers of the icy north.

Every year, in long and winding lines, we journey
further than any other animal on four legs.

With our wide and padded feet, we walk in each
other's footprints to keep out of the deep snow.

In spring, we move north to graze on lush
meadow grass. In autumn, we move south, where
we scrape through the snow to nibble on lichen.

Soon we will begin the journey again.

We are the **Common Toads**.

We journey through gardens and fields,
across streams and roads.

Every year, we make our way back to breed in
the pond where we once hatched from toad spawn.

We march in the cool, damp night.

We march across whatever's in our path.

We march together, a load of toads.

We are the **African Elephants**,
the giants of the savanna.

We march
through tall grasses,

swish, swish.

We march across the
dry earth, thump
thump.

Our matriarch leads the way. She is the oldest,
strongest female. She remembers where to
find water and food.

During the dry season, water holes are empty.
Many thirsty family groups join together into a huge herd.

We march onwards, until we finally
reach the river.

We are the Norway Lemmings.
We are busy, furry burrowers.

We live in the highlands and tundra of Norway.

We gnaw, we dig, we eat, we sleep, we have babies.

We have lots, and lots, and lots of babies.

Some years, when there is plenty
of food, there are too many babies.

Too many lemmings!

We need more space! More food!

Where shall we go?

We scurry out of our burrows and away,
searching for a new home.

We are the **Emperor Penguins**.
We live in a frozen world.

Come with us as we make our slow
shuffle across the frozen pack ice.

Our chicks are waiting to be fed.

Our mates are waiting for their
turn to make the long march
back to the sea to catch fish.

Nearly there!

We can see our colony!

Dots of black on a sheet of white!

We are the
Galapagos Land Iguanas.

We are the heat-seeking, dust-digging dragons.

We live on the lava fields of Fernandina,
a small and distant island.

When it's time to lay our eggs, we start the long, hard climb to the rim of a volcano.

There, we dig our nests in the soft ash. The volcano's heat will keep our eggs warm until they hatch.

We are the People of the world.
We travel to many places for many reasons.

We travel to find adventure.   We travel to find food.
We travel to find answers.   We travel to find freedom.

S. MARTIN

We travel to find safety.
We travel to find love.

We are the people.
We travel so far.

A Map of the World

Can you work out some of the journeys made by the animals in this book?

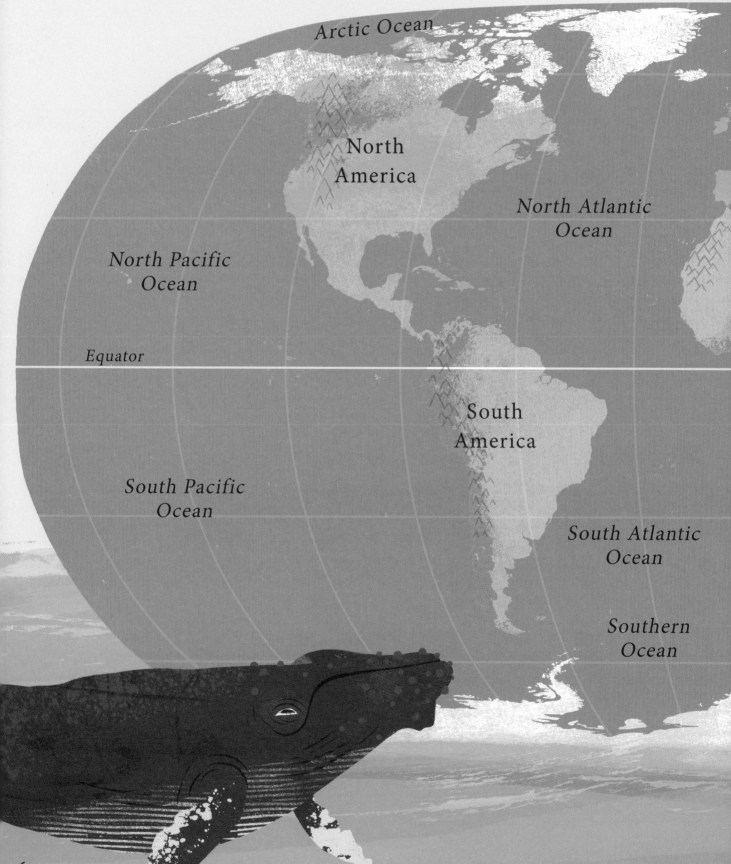

Arctic Ocean

North America

North Atlantic Ocean

North Pacific Ocean

Equator

South America

South Pacific Ocean

South Atlantic Ocean

Southern Ocean

Arctic Ocean

Europe

Asia

North Pacific
Ocean

Africa

Indian Ocean

Oceania

Southern
Ocean

Antarctica

Migration Data

Here you can find out the incredible distances traveled by each of the animals featured in this book.

Water migrations

LEATHERBACK TURTLE

DISTANCE TRAVELED: 10,00 miles (16,000 km) every year

MIGRATION: between warm breeding areas and cold feeding areas

RANGE: mainly tropical and temperate waters of the Atlantic, Pacific, and Indian Oceans, and Mediterranean Sea

CARIBBEAN SPINY LOBSTER

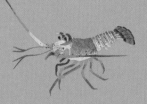

DISTANCE TRAVELED: up to 30 miles (50 km) each way

MIGRATION: from shallow coastal waters to deeper water in winter

RANGE: Caribbean, Gulf of Mexico, and western Atlantic Ocean, from North Carolina to Brazil

HUMPBACK WHALE

DISTANCE TRAVELED: 5,100 miles (8,200 km) each way

MIGRATION: from polar feeding areas in summer to tropical breeding areas in winter

RANGE: all oceans

ELEPHANT SEAL

DISTANCE TRAVELED: 13,000 miles (21,000 km) every year (males) and 11,000 miles (18,000 km) every year (females)

MIGRATION: out to open-sea feeding areas, returning to breeding sites on land in winter

RANGE: beaches and islands around California and Baja California, on the Pacific coast of North America

SOCKEYE SALMON

DISTANCE TRAVELED: more than 1,000 miles (1,600 km) upriver

MIGRATION: from open ocean, upriver to mate and lay eggs in lakes and streams

RANGE: Bering Sea to Japan, and Alaska to California

EUROPEAN EEL

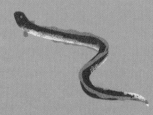

DISTANCE TRAVELED: up to 5,000 miles (8,000 km)

MIGRATION: adults swim from freshwater rivers and lakes in Europe, across to the Sargasso Sea in the western Atlantic Ocean. Larvae float back to the rivers on ocean currents.

Air migrations

RUBY-THROATED HUMMINGBIRD

DISTANCE TRAVELED: up to 3,700 miles (6,000 km) each way
MIGRATION: from summer breeding areas in eastern North America to wintering areas in Central America

WANDERING ALBATROSS

Record holder! Longest wingspan, at 11 feet (3.5 meters)
DISTANCE TRAVELED: up to 12,500 miles (20,000 km)
MIGRATION: can circumnavigate the globe around Antarctica, over the Southern Ocean, searching for food

MONARCH BUTTERFLY

DISTANCE TRAVELED: up to 3,000 miles (4,600 km)
MIGRATION:between breeding range in eastern United States and Canada and winter roosting sites in Mexico; also between breeding range in western United States and winter roosts in California

WHOOPING CRANE

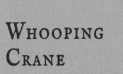

DISTANCE TRAVELED: up to 2,500 miles (4,000 km) each way
MIGRATION: between northern, inland breeding sites (main site is Wood Buffalo National Park, Canada) and southern, coastal wintering sites (main site is Aransas National Wildlife Refuge, Texas)

FRUIT BAT

DISTANCE TRAVELED: up to 1,250 miles (2,000 km) each way
MIGRATION: from breeding areas across equatorial Africa, out to northern and southern areas of Africa for around three months, to feed on seasonal fruit trees

BAR-HEADED GOOSE

DISTANCE TRAVELED: up to 5,000 miles (8,000 km)
Record holder! Highest recorded migration
MIGRATION ALTITUDE: more than 33,000 feet (10,000 m) over the Himalayan mountain range

DESERT LOCUST

DISTANCE TRAVELED: swarms can travel around 80 miles (130 km) per day, in a migration covering thousands of miles
MIGRATION: from their usual range in sub-Saharan Africa and the Middle East, out into the surrounding areas of Africa, southern Europe, and Asia

ARCTIC TERN

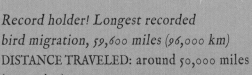

Record holder! Longest recorded bird migration, 59,600 miles (96,000 km)
DISTANCE TRAVELED: around 50,000 miles (80,500 km) every year
MIGRATION: between breeding grounds in the Arctic (during northern summertime) and Antarctica (during southern summertime)

Land migrations

ZEBRA

DISTANCE TRAVELED: up to 2,000 miles (3,200 km) each year
MIGRATION: a circular route following the rains of the Serengeti and Masai Mara regions of East Africa

WILDEBEEST

DISTANCE TRAVELED: up to 2,000 miles (3,200 km) each year
MIGRATION: a circular route following the rains of the Serengeti and Masai Mara regions of East Africa

POLAR BEAR

DISTANCE TRAVELED: up to 700 miles (1,125 km) each year
MIGRATION: between the frozen Arctic Ocean in winter and the tundra of northern Canada, Greenland, and Russia in summer

RED CRAB

DISTANCE TRAVELED: up to 2.5 miles (4 km) each way
MIGRATION: between inland rain forests and the coast of Christmas Island in the Indian Ocean

GARTER SNAKE

DISTANCE TRAVELED: around 12.5 miles (20 km) each way
MIGRATION: between winter hibernation dens and summer wetland habitat

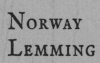

NORWAY LEMMING

DISTANCE TRAVELED: up to 100 miles (160 km)
MIGRATION: sudden explosion in numbers forces the lemmings to migrate to new, less populated areas. Migrations occur every three to five years

CARIBOU

Record holder! Longest land mammal migration
DISTANCE TRAVELED: up to 3,000 miles (5,000 km) each year
MIGRATION: north to tundra in spring and south to forests in winter
RANGE: Canada, Greenland, Alaska, northern Russia, and areas of Norway and Finland

COMMON TOAD

DISTANCE TRAVELED: between 165 feet (50 m) and 3 miles (5 km)
MIGRATION: between winter hibernation sites and breeding ponds

AFRICAN ELEPHANT

DISTANCE TRAVELED: several hundred miles
MIGRATION: with the seasons across the African savanna, in search of food, water, or mates

EMPEROR PENGUIN

DISTANCE TRAVELED: up to 100 miles (160 km) per trip
MIGRATION: between breeding colonies on the Antarctic ice sheets and ocean feeding areas

GALAPAGOS LAND IGUANA

DISTANCE TRAVELED: up to 10 miles (16 km) each way
MIGRATION: up to the crater of La Cumbre volcano, Fernandina Island, Galapagos, to lay eggs in the warm volcanic ash